AROUND THE WORLD IN 80 WAYS:
A lightweight guide to travel by the famous

A WEXAS PUBLICATION

£1 for each book sold will go to
Earthwatch

Earthwatch is an international charity
sponsoring 140 ecological projects around
the world, from Britain to Borneo, the
Arctic to Australia.

AROUND THE WORLD IN 80 WAYS:
A lightweight guide to travel by the famous

by Caroline Brandenburger with Carey Ogilvie

Illustrated by Paul Vickers

Published by WEXAS International

To C.

WEXAS International
45-49 Brompton Road
London SW3 1DE

ISBN 0-905802-06-3

Printed and bound in Great Britain by
BPCC Paperbacks Ltd
Member of BPCC Ltd

CONTENTS

Introduction

There is little worse than a travel bore. Their voice penetratingly holds forth at the dinner party, dropping names of far-flung places they've visited, "before it was discovered, of course". Stories follow of charming encounters with the natives in India, of that delightful little restaurant in a cobbled back-street in Provence, of the time they single-handedly fought off a boa constrictor in South America. By now, the other guests are sunk in apathetic gloom, and the hostess is in the kitchen drowning her sorrows with the sherry intended for the trifle.

Sometimes, however, there *is* a grain of wisdom to be gleaned. In *Around the World in 80 Ways*, we've asked over 80 well-travelled celebrities, from politicians to actors, from writers to explorers, to give their favourite travel tip or story. From favourite places, to their most vital piece of luggage, from what they miss most, to a favourite mode of transport.

One person who knows the science of travelling is the Queen. It seems she takes steel wardrobes and chests of drawers which are wheeled on and off the 'plane. These accompany the crates of Malvern water [avoid stomach upsets abroad by taking your own water supply], Oxford marmalade, Harrods' pork sausages [a favourite meal with Her Majesty and the Ladies in Waiting], a hot water bottle, down-filled pillows and, of course, a small kettle [monogrammed] and some English teabags [Earl Grey].

Whether a travelling monarch or a backpacker, we hope *Around the World in 80 Ways* finds a place in your luggage.

Caroline Brandenburger
Carey Ogilvie

1 Who goes where

To those who meditate Travel. —*Qualifications for a Traveller.* —If you have health, a great craving for adventure, at least a moderate fortune, and can set your heart on a definite object, which old travellers do not think impracticable, then —travel by all means.

Art of Travel by Francis Galton, 1872

JEFFREY BERNARD
Columnist

One of my favourite places is Sydney. It reminds me of the name of my column in *The Spectator*, 'Low Life'. There are very nice restaurants and bars, very nice people—open, and no bullshit. Whingeing pommies is what we are.

Russia depressed me tremendously, a gloomy bloody place, Russia. Though I'm sure the South is wonderful. Olga Korbut took me out for the day in Moscow, a sweet, delightful girl. She amused me by taking me to a restaurant in a forest outside Moscow. I was drinking vodka, and she said, I'm thinking of making a comeback, do you mind if I drink champagne? She drank three bottles. On the way back to Moscow on the motorway, we were stopped by two policemen with machine-guns. When she showed her identity card, they put down their machine-guns and brought out pencil and paper for her autograph.

TWIGGY
Model and actress

I don't like snakes, creepy crawlies, intense cold or height. Give me a warm beach, a shaded deck-chair, a long cool drink and I'm in my element. I like to be in the Caribbean, the Mediterranean, or even further afield, perhaps relaxing on the beaches of Goa. I don't mind hearing about other people's high adventures or watching them on film but for a holiday is always feet-up time. I have just finished a great read, *Zen in the Art of Climbing Mountains*, and enjoyed the philosophy and mountain adventure, but for me the experience has to be vicarious. Oh, I forgot to mention, preferably no telephones; I prefer the sun to be my watch and eat when my stomach dictates.

THE DUCHESS OF BEAUFORT
Chatelaine and fund-raiser

I would love to go back to China as the people are so charming, and it is such a vast country. I have only seen a small part, so much more to discover.

I went to China quite some years ago, when the Chinese people were not so used to seeing tourists, and as such they seemed rather frightened as I walked along. They would part in front of me like the Red Sea. When you laughed, they laughed, although they did not understand one word. I think you call it audience participation. I found the food good and simple, and eventually mastered the art of chopsticks, previously having gobbled it up any way possible.

I would also love to return the Galapagos Islands, where the animals are unique and unafraid of people. There is a wonderful saying for the Islands, "Don't touch the animals, but you can let the animals touch you." My fondest memories are of lying on the beaches with the seals, although there was one nasty moment when I was trapped by a rather large cow seal, which rolled over on top of me.

DONALD PLEASENCE
Actor

As a city kind of person, though I live partly in the country in France, New York has to be my favourite place. Because I've always been successful there, and had a great time. I first went with Laurence Olivier and Vivien Leigh in 1951. I went with a very small part, and I've been back four or five times to play the lead—it's quite something to be a star on Broadway. I love the city, and always

remember that first sight of it, coming in on a Cunard liner. I went on deck at six in the morning, and had that first glimpse from the Hudson River.

It's changed very little, ugly and beautiful at the same time. It's hardly on the side of ecology or clean air. I like the excitement of it, the cosmopolitan mix of people and cultures. As for food, you can get anything you like. I love American food—have done since the first moment I got there. We were still having rationing from the War, and the idea of stalls on the street selling hot dogs and hamburgers, being able to get bacon and eggs at four in the morning... We used to go down to the Village every night, where the cabaret was Eartha Kitt, and Harry Bela-fonte, and John Carradine reading the Bible! It was mar-vellous, and I've never changed my mind.

LUCINDA GREEN
3-Day Eventer

I love going to the Barrier Reef, scuba-diving and other water pursuits off a privately chartered vessel. The vessel we went on was called The Booby Bird and it slept approximately sixteen people. You take your own booze, catch your own food and have a week living with nature...

SUSAN GEORGE
Actress

My favourite holiday will always be to the mountains to ski. I like to drive rather than fly, visiting France and Switzerland en route to Austria. The best part is the last leg of the journey, that moment when you turn a corner and get the unbelievably beautiful 'first sight of snow'. I then become quite childlike, excited, giggly and desperate to get out of the car and be in it.

JOHN NETTLES
Actor

Cornwall is the best place in England to holiday. I am biased because I come from there, it is true, but go see, judge for yourself. The beauty of the place is matched only by the gentleness and impressively philosophic nature of the inhabitants illustrated by the following. I was lost in an obscure bit of the county and running out of petrol fast. An old weather-beaten Cornishman, chronicle of old time in tin and clay mine, was hoeing his garden by the side of the road. I stopped and asked him where the nearest petrol station might be.

"I don't know," replied he, looking gloomily to the ground. "But...", he brightened, "don't matter much, this road ends in half a mile."

SIR HUGH CASSON
Architect and artist

For my holidays I usually go to Greece where I was a student in 1932.

JON SNOW
Newscaster

I'm a bit of an oddball—I've been paid to travel so much, and if I'm honest, I tend to go to the antithesis of where I'm paid to go. Cape Cod, for instance, or the wilds of the west coast of Scotland. Occasionally I go back to places I've been to in a work context—Grenada or Chile—and see it differently. In Chile, the scenery is wonderful, and I intend to do Darwin's Trail, the Beagle Trail. Grenada, because it seems to me pretty near a Caribbean idyll.

Scotland is total escape and wilderness. I go there to

escape telephones and electronics. I'm not drawn to a place by books or films, but I am drawn by the absence of technological development. You have to walk or bike, there's no television to sate you children's interest, it's self-sufficiency. That is what's most important—getting away, relying on your own devices.

I can't bear the thought of a package holiday—I've never been on one. As a foreign reporter, the last time I looked at my passport, I'd been to over 90 countries. It gives you a tremendous impression of what's available, but blunts your appetite to go there. In Guatemala, a spectacularly beautiful country, with beautiful people, I stood in Guatemala City and thought, I would have paid to come here, and I've been paid to come here...

JEREMY IRONS

Actor

As for my favourite places in the world, I should like to draw a shroud of secrecy over them, since one of the reasons I love them is that they are not yet known to any but the most ardent traveller.

I try to find somewhere right off the beaten track, which includes a little danger, a good pinch of the unknown and, by not planning, leaves open the element of surprise.

LADY BROCKET

Businesswoman and former model

I'm torn between Italy and South America. But it's probably Italy. I love everything about it—the people, the way of life, and the variation. There are modern places like Milan, very similar to New York or London. Then down south, there's the wonderful sea, the food is so varied and good, the people very open and friendly. And they're cultured in an indirect way—either they study it, or they just seem to grow up with it. Even the children have style.

2 How they get there

Elephants.—They are expensive and delicate, but excellent beasts of burden, in rainy tropical countries. The traveller should make friends with the one he regularly rides, by giving it a piece of sugar-cane or banana before mounting.

Art of Travel by Francis Galton, 1872

GILES WATERFIELD
Director, The Dulwich Picture Gallery

My favourite mode of transport is train. It is the most relaxing experience one can have. I immediately fall asleep, and arrive feeling wonderful. It's the rhythm—I find it extremely soporific. But if you should want to read or write, like Trollope, who, I think, wrote most of his novels on a train, it's most stimulating to the brain.

The most curious journey I had was coming back from Washington, escorting paintings. I took them from Washington to Paris, and it took 36 hours. One painting was from Dulwich, and there were nineteen others, all by Watteau. I found myself sitting in a cargo 'plane, travelling overnight, with 20 paintings, with a total value of some 100 million. Plus two Irish horses, wonderful steeds, which were being transported for a race in Paris. The only passengers were a beautiful woman groom, and me, travelling through the night. We couldn't hear any noise from the pictures, but one could from the horses below in their vast metal boxes. There was the frightening thought that they might suddenly break loose and come thundering through into the cockpit.

ROBIN HANBURY-TENISON
Explorer, writer and campaigner for tribal peoples.

Horse or camel has to be my preferred way of travelling. A lot of it goes back to Wilfred Thesiger, who was the pioneer of thinking modern forms of transport were not a good thing. He is very purist about it. Years ago I talked to him and at the time regarded his views as reactionary, being so anti-mechanical. All my early expeditions were with jeeps, or down the Amazon in little boats with outboard motors at the back. I used to justify this by saying you could see more and stop when you wanted.

Now I've come round to saying that's not a very good way to travel. But horses are the ultimate. The five journeys I've had by horse, with my wife Louella, have confirmed it. Your hands are free to write, take notes, dictate into a hand-held machine. You can hear and see and smell the world in which you're travelling. Whereas if you're confined inside a car, you can't. If you're travelling, you're preoccupied with trivia. If it's on a horse, they're good and sensible trivia. If you're driving, you're preoccupied with fuel — can you get it?—and tyres wearing out. If you're on a horse, you're thinking about the availability of pasturage, hay, the condition of your horse's feet. You're closer to this interests of the people you're meeting. Everyone likes you on a horse.

JENNY AGUTTER
Actress

I never fly without ear-plugs, so that the droning of the 'plane doesn't stay in my ears after the flight (also to cut out the various other noises that occur to prevent sleep). I drink lots of water on the flight, but no alcohol. I put lots of oil on my face to counteract dryness and to make me look so unattractive that no-one wants to talk to me!

COLIN THUBRON
Travel Writer

I am happy with any mode of transport except boats and camels. Boats are wretched. You see little but water, feel miserable, and are condemned to whoever else was foolish enough to embark on one: generally the senile and very rich. It is no mystery at all to me why so many people commit suicide on boats. There's nothing preferable to do.

Camels, on the other hand, are ingeniously varied in punishing you for selecting them. Apart from a standard repertory of biting and kicking, they can spit gobs of green froth from great distances, with the accuracy of a Greek.

MAX HASTINGS
Editor, Daily Telegraph

Having travelled steerage for most of my working life, I always used to hanker for the glories of First Class. Now that I have got to the front of the 'plane, I can confidently report that all the interesting-looking people on every flight disappear smartly to the back. And all that expensive food and drink one is offered seems wasted, when the most experienced travellers are too old to eat a lot, and too sensible to drink much.

After fifteen years as a foreign correspondent, my strongest conviction is that one should never worry for a moment about looking foolish, but concentrate simply on being comfortable. Travelling in Economy on long 747 flights, I would appropriate all the blankets I could find, and stretch out on the floor anywhere there was room to sleep properly. The first rule for every traveller is to sleep whenever and wherever you get the chance, because there may not be another.

COL. JOHN BLASHFORD-SNELL
Explorer and founder of Operation Raleigh

My favourite mode of transport is elephants, without a doubt. Partly because I love elephants, and partly because they're very reliable. They don't make odorous fumes— well, they do sometimes, if they've got wind. But they're so intelligent, so strong. If you push leaves in one end, they carry on and on. In fact, they're the most intelligent animals I've ever come across—more than dogs or horses.

They defend you—we were attacked by a tiger in Nepal, and the elephant slammed its trunk, which is as strong as steel wire cable, and saw it off. They pick their way through the jungle, and if you drop something, they pick it up with their trunk and hand it back to you. They can be temperamental—the one I used has killed two people. But they can see their way across a river, and if there's a point that's dangerous, they won't go.

They're not that comfortable—six hours in the saddle makes you quite sore. I'm working on a design for a more comfortable howdah. And they all have different gaits. They look as if they're moving quite slowly, but if you get down and walk beside them, you have a problem keeping up.

And they talk to each other, with a very low sound which the human ear can't pick up. They are a constant source of fascination. I don't know why an animal with that size and strength bothers to be bossed around by mere mortals. But they seem to have an amazing affinity with humans.

DAVID BLUNKETT MP
Shadow Secretary of State for Health

My favourite means of transport is by tandem. With the wind in your face, with the smell of flowers and trees and with healthy exercise, who could wish for more—other than a sunny climate to go with it.

My worst means of transport is the London Underground. A crowded train, on a busy commuter line first thing in the morning is hot, smelly and slow. Breakdowns turn an unpleasant experience into a nightmare. With yesterday's garlic adding to those who forgot to get up early enough to have a shower.

ELSPETH HUXLEY
Writer

Most of my travel took place in a bygone age when it was unpredictable and a lot more fun. Nairobi to London took six days if you were lucky, more if you weren't. You travelled in a four-engine biplane called Hengist or Horsa, maximum speed about 120mph, and came down for the night at primitive rest-houses along the banks of the Nile—on one occasion in the desert, for several nights, waiting for a spare part to come from Cairo. A hospitable detachment of the Egyptian army manoeuvres took us in. A Belgian fellow passenger with his own whisky supply sozzled all day, snored loudly all night and broke frequently into raucous and obscene song; the Egyptian officers, strict Muslims and very correct, were deeply offended, the rest of us embarrassed, communication difficult and the temperature about 110°F in the shade. The aeroplane, duly repaired, disgorged us at Brindisi where we got into a train to Paris, and ended with our fight against fierce head-winds over the Channel in competition with a fishing boat battling with the waves below; the fishing boat won.

SIR COLIN MARSHALL
Chairman of British Airways

Having been involved in shipping, car rental and air transport, virtually all my whole career has been spent on the move. Nowadays I am mostly in the air and I do enjoy the environment that air travel provides to actually read, rather than skim, correspondence and reports of one kind or another. To a business person, that is relaxation itself. My first love, the sea, hardly gets a look in apart from those times in Hong Kong, for instance, when I can dispense with the car and jump on the Star Ferry to join

the jostling crowds taking the age-old trip across the harbour between Victoria and Kowloon. The short trip in perspective. Apart from that, I suppose my favourite form of transport is the escalators at Heathrow and Gatwick, from where I can get a bird's eye view of the way business is going and how our customers are being served in the busy terminals!

ROGER BLACK
Olympic sprinter

My favourite mode of transport is in fact a taxi, especially in New York or London. I love the freedom one has to really look at and get the feel of a major city from a taxi. I hate driving (which probably explains my love of being driven by taxi) and also enjoy the varied conversations that a taxi driver can have with one.

I must warn any prospective traveller to New York to be prepared for a hair-raising experience in the back of a Yellow Cab, since New Yorkers are not known for their patience or manners behind the wheel.

A.S. BYATT
Novelist

I will pay any amount of money to go on an aeroplane without a film showing. There must be a club of us who don't want to be made to watch a film like small children. The air stewardesses are like school-mistresses, tapping the windows to make you close them. I went to Australia—I'll probably never see it again—and this b***** woman came and tapped on the window and said, 'Some people want to watch the film!' It's a form of tyranny. It's physically very unpleasant, visually very poor quality, and the sound is frightful. I can't see for whose convenience it is. I find it's a real invasion of my body and my mind. It's like being back at boarding-school. What I want is space for my legs, and a neck-rest for where my head is, not where it isn't.

MARQUESS OF BATH
Landowner and artist

One disastrous thing I once took with me (on travels through South America in 1960) was a car with automatic transmission. Whenever it broke down, I had the experience of (e.g. Colombian) mechanics pulling the whole mechanism to pieces, and then asking me how to fit it together again. I was someone who, when tested for my 'Mechanical Aptitude' before doing my Army National Service in 1950, obtained a score of 0/6.

DIANA RIGG
Actress

I got the best tip about how to counteract jet lag from a steward aboard British Airways. While on board, eat as little as possible and drink as much as possible, preferably non-alcoholic. Sounds dull, but it works.

JOHN LE CARRÉ
Novelist

I walk. My walks are what teeth are to dogs. When I can't walk any more, I won't know the world any more. The best walks are in Cornwall and the best of all from Portcurno to my house, which lies on the Cornish coastal footpath. When I'm away from home I have one dream: arriving back at Tregiffian with my face tingling from the wind and my tongue tasting sea-salt and eating boiled eggs for high tea.

JULIET STEVENSON
Actress

The form of transport I have most enjoyed was camel riding in the Sahara Desert. It's a perfect speed at which to travel and you feel as high as though you were flying, but without the drawbacks of ear-popping, seat-belts, and turbulence trauma.

JEFFREY BERNARD
Columnist

My favourite way of travel is the riverboat. I've been down the Nile, and up the Mississippi. It's so relaxing and peaceful, unlike the Cross Channel ferry. There are no yobs on the Nile or the Mississippi. I've been along the river in Bangkok, and in Spain from Seville which goes to the sea near Cadiz. I like rivers very much, and most boats have excellent food.

Otherwise by train —with a really good restaurant car and bar. That's essential. The most awful way to travel is by car or by 'plane, it's so contained.

SARAH MILES
Actress

For me, the only way to travel nowadays is with my husband, Robert Bolt. Being paralysed down his right side from a stroke, we always get spoilt at airports, and go to the aeroplane by ambulance. It's such a privilege—I'd certainly never travel without him—!

SIR VIVIAN FUCHS

Explorer and geologist

Driving a sledge with a nine-dog team on a clear day is exhilarating, and I was lucky to travel thousands of miles during two years with my very intelligent Leader 'Darkie'.

But he had a will of his own, as on the occasion when I left the sledge to talk to another driver. Suddenly he started off on his own, and led the team on a wide arc around two icebergs, finally finding and turning along the tracks we had made when arriving.

Two hours later my companion and I, with his team, found ourselves back at the camp site we had left that morning. We found Darkie and his team sitting quietly awaiting our arrival!

I feel sure that they felt great satisfaction at having done so well. Unhappily, we should have arrived back at our Base hut in the opposite direction.

3 Who speaks what

Good Interpreters are very important: men who would have been used by their chiefs, missionaries, &c., as interpreters, are much to be preferred.

Signals.—If flashing signals are needed, anything may be used for signalling, that appears and disappears, like a lantern, or an opened and closed umbrella, or that moves, as a waved flag or a person walking to and fro on the crest of a hill against the sky. Sound also can be employed, as long and short whistles. Their use can be thoroughly taught in two hours, and however small the practice of the operators, communication, though slow, is fairly accurate, while in practised hands its rapidity is astonishing.

Art of Travel by Francis Galton, 1872

LORD HUNT
Mountaineer, soldier, leader of the 1953 Everest Expedition

In 1962 I was asked—a very great privilege—to be leader of a joint British-Soviet expedition to Tajikistan. This expedition, from the British point of view, was joint English-Scottish, with an equivalent number of Soviets.

There was a serious problem of language, some of us tried very hard with our Russian, and the Russians, under orders, tried very hard with their English.

We had a planning meeting at base camp, at the foot of a glacier. There was a great problem with getting heavy equipment and supplies up the mountain. We didn't have any Sherpas, and would have had to hump it up the mountain ourselves. We had to persuade the Russian helicopter pilot to go much higher than he ever normally flew, to drop the supplies down. He stood shaking his head, and we tried hard to persuade him.

What tipped the balance was when a Scottish member of the team opened a crate of his national drink—whisky—and waved two bottles at him. It didn't need any language to persuade him to jump into his helicopter and fly it right up high and drop the supplies.

CLARE RAYNER
Agony Aunt

I was staying in a Corsican hotel, washed my hair, and couldn't find a hairdryer in my room. I couldn't for the life of me remember the French for hairdryer (I suppose it's *cheveux au sec*, or something of that order), so I decided to go up to reception with my head wrapped in a towel, to ask them directly for what I needed. I had a brain-wave when I arrived at the desk, and I asked for a *"vent chaude"*; I thought this was a very good description of what a hairdryer provides—hot air. But what I didn't know, of course, was that in French that means a hot fart. They eventually worked out what it was I needed and provided it and I became a very popular guest in the hotel because I spoke French so interestingly.

SIR JOHN HARVEY-JONES
Industrialist

If travelling, it is wise to ensure that you speak the language of the airline on which you travel. On one occasion, I flew TAP from London via Biarritz to Lisbon—or so I thought. I was sitting sleepily contemplating Biarritz in darkness and watching new passengers embarking when my eye caught a neon sign saying Lisbon. I got off the 'plane just as the doors were closing—just as well, for the next stop was Brazil. All the announcements had been made in Portuguese—and the flight schedule had been unexpectedly changed. There are real advantages to flying 'planes where you speak the language.

MILES KINGTON
Columnist and writer

When I was in Burma in 1987, working on a Great Journeys' film for the BBC, I received an invaluable linguistic hint from Tom Owen Edmunds, the travel photographer who was doing the stills photos for the book the BBC wanted to do for the series.

We had a day off at Inle Lake, the strange upcountry lake where fisherman operate their oars with one leg, and where whole villages are built of floating vegetation. In one of these villages he and I and my wife were followed everywhere by crowds of little children who insisted on singing "Frere Jacques" to us, and then asking for money. (We had *Frere Jacques* sung to us by children more than any other song in Burma, and we never found out where they learnt it). Finally Tom had had enough.

"Right," he said, "there's only one thing to do. We'll sing to them."

"Fair enough," I said. "Sing what?" "*Jerusalem*," he said. "Know the words? 'And did those feet in ancient time' etc?"

"I know the tune," I said. "It was drummed into us at school. But the words... It was a long time ago."

"Never mind," said Tom. "I've got the words with me." And blow me down, he produced a small piece of paper from his safari jacket with all the words of *Jerusalem* on it, and we sang it all the way through so lustily that by the end not a child was left within sight, partly because my wife was asking them for money now.

How come, I asked him afterwards, he happened to have the words..?

"Well, I've been in so many bars and places around the world where people sing you their songs, and eventually say to you, 'Now you sing a song from your country!', and I can never think of one. So finally I decided to take the words of one with me wherever I went, and *Jerusalem* is one that seems to go down best..."

A wonderful piece of advice. I've never taken it, but it's still a wonderful piece of advice.

4 Who deals where

General Remarks. —A frank, joking, but determined manner, joined with an air of showing more confidence in the good faith of the natives than you really feel, is the best.

Art of Travel by Francis Galton, 1872

PAUL SMITH
Fashion designer

I signed papers for a £1 million freehold property in a field in Italy—my solicitor flew out from England for an hour to sign the papers. He sent me a postcard later saying, "All the papers are now complete. I enjoyed my Luton for breakfast, Lucca for lunch and London for supper."

RT HON THE BARONESS CHALKER OF WALLASEY
Minister for Overseas Development

I think the most obscure place where I have had a business meeting must have been in a sand-bagged encampment deep in the heart of Uganda. I sat with the President of Uganda under a mango tree for over two hours, near Kumi. This was the headquarters of his field camp in the region, to which he had gone to try to bring people together and stop civil unrest. The only disturbance was from small, unripe mangos falling from the tree. I had to wait until I got to the market in Kampala before I could buy a mango to eat.

My best tip is always take anti-mosquito spray, for you never know where you will sit or for how long, at a meeting in Africa.

MAX HASTINGS
Editor, Daily Telegraph

If you are on holiday, be as brave as you like about what you eat and drink. But, if you are travelling to work, and your first job is to stay on your feet, then don't worry about how foolish you look drinking bottled water, and refusing the sheep's eyes.

5 Who packs what

Stores for Individual Use

For each man (independently of duration of journey):-

Clothes; mackintosh rug, ditto sheet; blanket-bag; spare blanket.

Share of plates, knives, forks, spoons, pannikins, or bowls.

Share of cooking-things, iron pots, coffee-mill, &c.

Spare knife, flints, steel, tinder-box, tinder, four pipes.

Bags, 6lbs.

Provisions for emergency —Five days of jerked meat, at 3lbs a day (on average).

Two quarts of water (on average), 4lbs; share of kegs, 1lb.

Art of Travel by Francis Galton, 1872

MAX HASTINGS
Editor, The Daily Telegraph

The only indispensable baggage for any traveller is a book, the bigger the better. My claims to any sort of literacy rest not upon anything I have learned at school, but upon years of sitting alone in 'planes, hotel dining-rooms and bunkers reading Trollope, Dickens, Jane Austen, George Eliot— anything to put my mind as far as possible from the uncomfortable realities around me. Nothing can match the companionship, nor command the affection in adversity, of a good book. I can never understand why so many people rely upon airport bookstalls to supply travel reading. Before I go abroad, I take far more care choosing the books I shall take from my own shelves or from the library than I do on my clothes. Very often, if I am going to be away for weeks, half the weight in my suitcase is made up of books.

For the rest, I take much less trouble about deciding what to take with me, than about what to leave behind. Even I am only going to Paris for the weekend, I leave my wallet, diary, every kind of valuables except one credit card, so that if my room is robbed, I have a minimum to lose and replace. I take my cheapest camera. I use only very old and very cheap luggage for travelling on 'planes.

COL. JOHN BLASHFORD-SNELL
Explorer and founder of Operation Raleigh

I always take a pen-knife, a Swiss army knife. It's invaluable for everything - taking thorns out of an elephant's foot, hacking through the jungle, opening a can of beans, repairing things. I'd never travel without it.

GENERAL SIR JOHN HACKETT
Soldier and historian

The one thing I always take with me—is the thought of coming home. I always travel hopefully, with the thought of coming home as the light at the end of the tunnel. I've lived for thirty years in homes belonging to the Sovereign as a soldier, to a university as Vice-Chancellor, and only in the last thirteen years lived in our own home, an ancient mill-house in the Cotswolds. Home is where you're among people of your own kind, with the ability to feel at ease.

After the Battle of Arnhem, I was in hiding, very badly wounded. In all that time, my wife knew I was alive, but that I was in very poor shape. She couldn't tell anyone that I was alive, even the War Office didn't know I was alive. They like to tie things up, and after four months they post you 'Presumed Killed'. After four months they duly did so. Three weeks later I returned. My dear wife was only a widow for three weeks, because I was escaping in a canoe down the Rhine. Three weeks was enough time for friends to write in and say how sorry they were. And then I turned up. One of them asked for his letter back. "If I'd known the fellow was going to turn up again, I'd never have said all those things about him!" All that time, the thought of home was very important to me.

It doesn't prevent you from going all over the earth. I was born in Australia, and though I lived there until I went to Oxford, I never regarded myself as an Australian. I thought that Australia was an ante-room to elsewhere. I felt that Britain was my home, and felt at home with the British way.

TERRY O'NEILL
Photographer

I stuff my pockets with film 'cos I don't trust those airport x-ray machines. 'Film safe' or not, I'd have looked a bit of a twerp if, after flying to LA especially to shoot Jodie Foster, I'd turned out a load of foggy pictures.

DAME BARBARA CARTLAND
Novelist

If you have false jewellery, it always shows when you go through the luggage control, which is an awful bore. Wrap it up in that silver baking—what do you call it?—silver foil. It won't show up then. But it doesn't seem to work with real jewellery.

FREDERICK FORSYTH
Thriller writer

While the developed world of North-West Europe and America may become increasingly and more virulently opposed to the idea of smoking cigarettes, this fetish has certainly failed to penetrate into Third World or, indeed, before the end of Communism, behind the Iron Curtain. After years of travelling through Eastern Europe and various parts of the Middle East, Africa and Asia, I have found that the best lubricant for taxi drivers, Customs officials, and various others with whom one may need to make a friendly rather than formal contact, is the ability to be able to offer a carton of English cigarettes. In many parts of the world they form a kind of currency second only to the American dollar. As a result, I always carry a few!

LIZ McCOLGAN
Olympic long -distance runner

I always take a packet of porridge and a bunch of bananas.

KATIE BOYLE
Agony Aunt

Having been an agony aunt all my life, and therefore practical, I can say that no clothes will crease if you pack with plastic as our grandparents used to pack with tissue. I use dry-cleaning bags, as they're so light-weight. I was given the tip years ago, when plastic wasn't used very much, by the editor of the Vogue Beauty Book. I was going to Australia to model for them and it worked like a dream. No rushing around for irons at all.

A.S. BYATT
Novelist

One thing I always take, apart from books which are absolutely essential, is Johnson's Baby Powder. Because when you're travelling, you get all hot and sticky, and often can't find a shower. It's not strongly perfumed like the others, and has a comforting smell. A toothbrush is important too, though you can improvise a toothbrush, while you can't improvise books.

I'm not interested in Marmite, or digestive biscuits. It would take me a few years to get worked up about those. It's a peculiarly English thing to do so, and I don't travel to be peculiarly English.

ROBERT ELMS
TV Presenter

I always take a short-wave radio and a huge list of frequencies so that if I'm somewhere like Guyana, I know how to tune in to the World Service.

LIZA GODDARD
Actress

Take one of those aerated spoons for making tea and some good tea. So often the tea is inferior in hotels.

NICHOLAS PARSONS
TV and radio presenter

If you travel with a mobile 'phone, or pocket recording machine, do not pack them in your main luggage. They look very suspicious if your suitcase is one of those scanned before going into the hold, and that piece of luggage can be delayed and opened for examination— a most unpleasant experience. Always carry such items in your hand luggage.

MARK OTTAWAY
Travel Correspondent, The Sunday Times

I am a hopeless packer. Everyone sees me going off with huge great suitcases, and they say, Someone who travels as much as you ought to be able to pack better. And my truthful answer, or at least, 90 per cent truthful, is that it's because I travel so much, I know how much not having one tiny thing, whether it's an aspirin or a plaster or a torch, can totally ruin a trip. If I went to the Greek Islands without my goggles, or skiing without my sunglasses...

JONATHAN ROSS
TV Presenter

I pack plenty of hardware: an Applemac computer, a CD Walkman, loads of classical CDs, a miniature TV, and that most important item, travel insurance.

MICHAEL FISH
Weathercaster

An umbrella is the one thing a weatherman should never be caught unexpectedly without by the public. But due to the fact that nature has thinned my hair somewhat, I never go anywhere without one of those silly little cloth caps—a baseball cap. Many years ago, I went to Egypt in the middle of winter, and found myself caught out. Holidays are usually restricted in time and in cost nowadays, so I don't tend to find myself in places without a cultural understanding of the baseball cap. It's a BBC one, probably because it was a freeby, and it doesn't get blown off, which is an advantage over the panama.

HUGO VICKERS
Biographer

The one thing I must take when I travel is my diary, which I write. I've been keeping it day to day since May 1976, and I've now got several shelves of them, and hundreds of volumes. I like being able to keep things, not lose things—a day should be kept and lived, not lived and lost. I take the Mae West line— if you keep a diary, one day it'll keep you. It tells the story as you see it at the very moment. So you can look back and see how it was, rather than building on it as time goes by.

I'm always behind, and trying to catch up. I once wrote thirty pages about one day. It's very honest. I use it as my best friend, and tell it things I wouldn't tell my friends. If I'm on a flight, I won't take a book, I'll take my diary and catch up. And when I am actually travelling, it's a way of isolating yourself from other people. If you're scribbling away in your diary, people don't come up and bother you.

SIMON HEFFER
Deputy Editor, The Spectator

I never travel without my panama, because I get sunburnt. I've got a very big one, bought for me by my wife in Jermyn Street, about three-foot wide, and it puts my entire body in the shade. It's been around the world - Africa, Australia and Asia, and I wouldn't like to be without it. I still managed to get malaria wearing the hat though - the mosquitoes got my forehead just below the hat.

KAREN DIXON
3-day Eventer

Always mark your luggage clearly, this really is important. At the Seoul Olympics we were all given identical suitcases—everyone had them and no name tags. On arriving at Seoul Airport there were 350 identical suitcases going around and around with no tags and nobody knew whose was whose—what a nightmare. We had to open all suitcases to see who was rider, who was rower. So mark your luggage clearly.

NANETTE NEWMAN
Actress

If, like me, you hate packing and unpacking, try this to

make it less horrid. Pack all your clothes on paddedhangers, making sure that you surround the hook bit with lots of tissue paper. Use T-shirts, underwear, sweaters, etc. to stuff inside jackets and blouses. You can upack really speedily—just hang everything up straight out of the suitcase, and it saves you ringing down for more hangers (as there never seem to be enough), and when you leave, repacking is much simpler. Don't use wire hangers because they poke into everything.

Last year I had to spend three weeks travelling around staying at a different hotel each night - and this system of packing saved my sanity!

LUCY IRVINE
Author and castaway

I never go anywhere without a notepad and two pens—in case one expires mid-sentence—a picture of my three children and, strange as it may seem, a nutmeg. It's a kind of lucky charm to replace my St. Christopher which I accidently left on Tuin. Another thing which you must never be without when you travel is an open mind. I wonder if that counts as hand luggage?

6 Who wears what

Clothing.—There are such infinite varieties of dress, that I shall only attempt a few general remarks and give a single costume, that a traveller of great experience had used to his complete satisfaction. The military authorities of different nations have long made it their study, to combine in the best manner the requirements of handsome effect, of cheapness, and of serviceability in all climates.

Art of Travel by Francis Galton, 1872

MARQUESS OF BATH
Landowner and artist

I am not really an appropriate member of the public to question on the matter of clothing abroad, in that I am far too 'stay-at-home' nowadays. But when I did travel, it was always necessary to carry a colourful headband, both to express my identity and also to prevent my long hair getting in my eyes, or tied up into overhead branches, Absalom fashion.

EMILY LLOYD
Actress

I never go anywhere without a pair of white pants from Marks and Spencer - everyone always needs a clean pair.

DRUSILLA BEYFUS
Journalist and author

I resist the temptation to take any jewellery of personal value as it is just one other thing to think about.

An exception, because I feel lost without it, is my gold ring set by Wendy Ramshaw, a practising British designer. The piece consists of four separate rings that can be juggled with to form different geometric patterns on the finger. One may twiddle the bands like worry beads. The rings are decorative, can be worn night and day and provide a token cheer-up to the most dismal hotel dressing-table. When unworn, the rings fit an assigned stand and turn into sculpture.

VIVIENNE WESTWOOD
Fashion designer

I like wearing a safari suit for shooting tigers in.

MAX HASTINGS
Editor, The Daily Telegraph

If it is a long haul flight, I always travel in jeans and slacks rather than ruin a good suit. Unless you think it is worth impressing the airline stewardess with your Savile Row tailoring, good clothes are a waste of time on aircraft.

NICK FALDO
Golfer

While travelling I always wear my Audemars Piguet watch and I take pairs of jeans to relax in.

CHRISTOPHER BIGGINS
TV presenter

I always travel with either a bright red or blue Mickey Mouse T-shirt. As I sleep with nothing on at home, in an emergency, I don't want to frighten anyone.

JOAN COLLINS
Actress

If I am going on a long 'plane journey, I slip into my silk lounging pyjamas.

PAUL SMITH
Fashion designer

If you are taking a suit on holiday, cotton or linen are best for a hot climate. It's bound to arrive creased so, did you know that if you fill a bath full of hot, steamy water and hang a suit on a hanger in the bathroom for as long as you can, you will have a soaking wet suit without a single crease? No, seriously, it really does work!

NICHOLAS COLERIDGE
Managing Director, Condé Nast Publications

I never go anywhere, however hot or remote, without a cashmere cardigan and tie. I find that, in the midst of roughing it, it rather raises the spirits to smarten up at the end of the day, though I don't necessarily wear the cardigan and the tie together.

7 Who buys what

Payment.—Speaking of presents and articles for payment, as of money, it is essential to have a great quantity and variety of *small change*, wherewith the traveller can pay for small services, for carrying messages, for draughts of milk, pieces of meat, &c. Beads, shells, tobacco, needles, awls, spear, cotton caps, handkerchiefs, clasp-knives, small axes, spear and arrow heads, generally answer this purpose.

Art of Travel by Francis Galton, 1872

DAVID WICKERS
Travel Correspondent, The Sunday Times

I once needed a nut and bolt in Greece (I won't bore you with the reasons except to say they were nautical and necessary). I found a hardware store stuffed to the gills with all manner of miscellaneous thingumajigs and a dead cert for a nut and bolt. I slowly described (in English) and gesticulated (in Greek) my needs but received a blank stare from the man behind the counter. I drew (in biro) what I needed. The man beamed a look of total recognition, toddled off into the dusty bowels of the shop and came back with a table lamp.

MAUREEN LIPMAN
Actress and journalist

In 1963 I went to Israel for the first time with a party of young people led by a diminutive gentleman called Arthur the Organiser. This was a misnomer. Arthur's great contribution to our trip to the Holy Land was to mislay the return tickets, which meant travelling by steerage to Milan and then from Milan to Calais standing in a train. My present to my parents from Israel was a painting 3ft x 2ft. It was not a pleasant journey.

8 Who likes a luxury

Luxuries.—The luxuries and elegances practicable in tent-life, are only limited by the means of transport. Julius Caesar, who was a great campaigner, carried parquets of wooden mosaic for his floors! The articles that make the most show for their weight, are handsome rugs, and skins, and pillows; canteens of dinner and coffee services; and candles, with screens of glass, or other arrangements to prevent them from flickering. The art of luxurious tenting is better understood in Persia than in any other country, even than in India.

Art of Travel by Francis Galton, 1872

JOSS ACKLAND

Actor

I always take 3 luxuries with me when I travel, the first being my wife, the second being jars of green olives stuffed with anchovies, chiles, and garlic from the shop Camisa— I even take jars to Italy, believe it or not.

My third luxury, is an expresso coffee machine—I take it everywhere, despite the heavy weight. You see, I love coffee and I am a coffee snob and American coffee drives me wild. You can't get good coffee anywhere—so I take my own.

VANESSA DE LISLE

Fashion adviser

I take a baby pillow and cashmere blanket for sleeping in Delhi airport, but most important is my big floppy Patricia Underwood straw hat.

LORD SNOWDON

Photographer

I recommend taking a jar of Marmite, as it stops you getting ill from foreign foods. It's good with hot water as well as on bread, and it's comforting.

DRUSILLA BEYFUS

Journalist and author

I always chuck in a pot of Countess Czaky's Collagen and Vitamin E cream, which I find the next best thing to a miracle cure for a dehydrated or jet-lagged complexion. I rub it in before having a bath, and afterwards my skin feels as if it has been fed on caviare.

DAME BARBARA CARTLAND
Novelist

I always take Ginseng with me—it completely stops jet-lag. You must have the Ginseng that comes from the North of China, it is frightfully expensive, but the American Ginseng is not so good. I've been taking it ever since Kitchener took it—everyone said, How marvellous, he never seems to be tired, and it was the Ginseng.

I always take a spoonful, and I've never run out of it. I tell everyone all over the world about it as most people don't know. It's the best tip I can give you—everyone flies nowadays, and they end up with that awful feeling— you know, as if you were walking on the moon. In fact, in America, astronauts *have* to take Ginseng.

LORD ARCHER OF WESTON-SUPER-MARE
Writer and former politician

Most of my travelling is done by car to far-flung constituencies. My one luxury for these journeys is a small swan feather pillow which my wife gave me, it is wonderfully soft—I am very lucky: I have a good driver and a soft pillow.

When I check into a hotel, I always check the pillows. I can't bear those hard pillows you get in some hotels, especially the ones that you can get in Germany.

"Vhot?—Lord Archer, you vont to have sovt pillow to puff up? Vhot is wrong with this nice hard one?"

I am not really a luxury man, I prefer the simple things in life. A lot of people who have made money then love the luxuries that can then be afforded. I prefer the simple life, preferring home-made Shepherd's Pie to the latest Nouvelle Cuisine. I like my comfort food.

For presents, I always take a square of cheddar cheese made by Alvis Brothers. It is the best present you

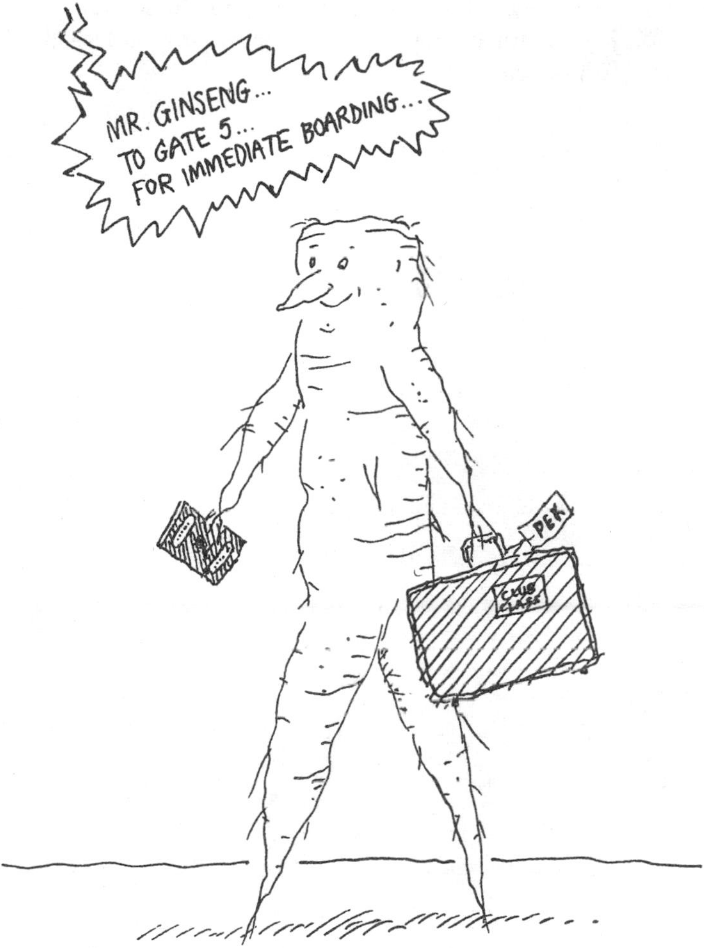
MR. GINSENG...
TO GATE 5...
FOR IMMEDIATE BOARDING...
PEK
CLUB CLASS

can give for it is definitely the finest cheddar cheese. It comes from the Cheddar Valley, and once you have tasted it, well— no other cheddar tastes quite the same.

My dream luxury, is quite simply—a good seat at any Test match.

9 Who reads what

Stationery.—Two ledgers; a dozen notebooks (see chapter on Memoranda and Log-Books); paper.

Ink; pens, pencils; sealing-wax; gum.

Board to write upon.

Books to read, say equal to six vols. the ordinary size of novels; and maps.

Bags and cases.

Sketching-books, colours, and pencils.

Art of Travel by Francis Galton, 1872

A.S.BYATT
Novelist

The only thing I must take is books. I become demented if I find myself alone in a place without reading matter. I got stuck in Bahrain for twenty-four hours, and stayed quite calm, sitting in my hotel room with a large plastic bag full of books. I take two kinds of book—one very difficult, and the other a very gripping narative, so that if the flight is terrible or the person sitting next to you is dreadful, you can get stuck in to it.

On my next journey, I'll take about 65 or 70 books, and in my hand luggage I'll take about three—and a big note book. Though since one was stolen in Rome, I've got rather nervous about it. Someone bashed in my rear window, and then roared off on a motorbike at 100mph and was never seen again.

SIR HUGH CASSON
Architect and artist

About 40 years ago I was asked to join a small 'Cultural Delegation' going to Peking to present to the Chinese Government at their request a document explaining the wish of the UK to resume the intellectual contacts broken by the War.

We were six in number including Stanley Spencer and Frederick Ayer. None of us had ever met. In those days the only way to reach China was via Moscow and across Siberia. Intourist confusion delayed us happily in Moscow until seats were found and off we went. The Aeroflot aircraft (twin-engined Dakota-like in appearance) landed every few hours for meals on the ground. As darkness fell, we landed and were conducted to 30-bed dormitories. Outside blizzards raged, inside Stanley Spencer played the upright piano often found in the

lounges.

Our last Soviet night was spent in Irkutsk where Royal rebels were sent for everlasting exile and next morning we landed at Ulan Bator. A small airport hardly bigger than a filling station, camels instead of taxis, but on a chenille-covered table in the centre of the departure lounge rested a book.

I grabbed it. It was one of those famous girls' school stories written in the twenties by Angela Brazil— and in good condition. How? Why? When? We left it behind in a pool of puzzlement.

IMOGEN STUBBS
Actress

I have always adored travel books. When I was trapped in Stratford-Upon-Avon with the RSC, I used to sneak Dervla Murphy books into rehearsals, and hang around travel shops dreaming of trekking across the Himalayas with only a small child, a donkey and, if possible, Bruce Chatwin for company. I yearned to stumble across some undiscovered tribe who would give us nice yoghurty drinks, rebaptise us under some startlingly wonderful waterfall, and reveal to us the mystery of the universe in sign language.

The wretched thing is that now that I am free and have enough money and the requisite child, I realize there is one huge obstacle to my embarking on such a journey—I am such a hypochondriac that the mere thought of having a tummy bug without a nearby Boots makes me feel unwell. The most wretched thing, however, is that Bruce Chatwin is no longer alive—and I fear he really was the *sine qua non* of my adventure.

TERRY WOGAN
TV Presenter

I don't think I would ever go away on holiday if I was only allowed to take one book away with me.

I've been trying to finish *War and Peace* for ten years. Now I've forgotten the beginning I'll have to start all over again. I read Myles Ma Glopalen in Spain and *Don Quixote* in Ireland. But Wodehouse, well, Wodehouse I'll read anywhere.

KEITH WATERHOUSE
Writer

The general assumption is that airport novels are meant to be started on the areoplane and finished on the beach. They are not. They are intended to be ploughed through at the airport itself, to fill in the endless waiting. That's why they're called airport novels.

RT HON ENOCH POWELL
Former politician

On my annual holiday, which is invariably spent in one region or another in France, I have for many years been accompanied habitually by an instalment of the mammoth novel series by Balzac or Zola.

JILLY COOPER
Writer

When I go away, I always take a novel by Barbara Pym or one by Anthony Trollope because they are so wonderfully comforting in that they remind me of England. And however lovely a holiday I have, I always get a bit homesick for England and long to come home again. My favourite Barbara Pym novel would be *Excellent Women* and my favourite Trollope is *Barchester Towers*.

A Trollope novel saved my sanity when I went on a trip to Death Valley and Monument Valley in America with a video crew, a film crew, a photographic crew, Patrick Lichfield, three very beautiful nude models, a make-up girl, stylist, a gloriously camp make-up man, and a location manager. We were all trying to photograph the Unipart calender and the rows between the various crews were absolutely pyrotechnic! It was great fun and wonderful copy and when everything became too much I retreated to my room into Anthony Trollope.

RT HON PADDY ASHDOWN MP
Leader of the Liberal Democrats

The one book I would like to take with me when travelling abroad is a collection of poems by John Donne. The book was given to me by my wife and I carried it with me whilst I was a soldier in the Far East. I particularly enjoy John Donne's poems because they have wit, artifice and passion about things both profane and sacred.

SIR HUGH CASSON
Architect and artist

If it is not a 'cheat' the book I would unhesitatingly take would be a huge sketchbook so I can write and illustrate my own travel story.

10 Who misses what

General Remarks.—Interest yourself chiefly in the progress of your journey, and do not look forward to its end with eagerness. It is better to think of a return to civilisation, not as an end to hardship and a haven from ill, but as a close to an adventurous and pleasant life.

Art of Travel by Francis Galton, 1872

LORD HUNT
Mountaineer, soldier, leader of the 1953 Everest expedition

I miss my wife and family—that sounds awfully trite. I enjoy having my wife with me, but for the twenty years that she was bringing up the children, she could not come too. If you take the Everest expedition as an example, she could not come, and I always missed her.

JAN MORRIS
Writer

Oh, without question what I miss most is my cat. I do see the logistical disadvantages of taking him around with me, and so does he—he has heard about British quarantine regulations. Still, I pine for his amused and sceptical company, not to mention the warm smell of him. I have often suggested to hoteliers that they offer cats as amenities—"Would you prefer", the receptionist would say when you checked in, " a room with or without a cat?"

When I asked the manager of a particularly suave Hong Kong hotel if I couldn't have one on my next visit, along with the hi-fi, fax machine and video library already provided, he seemed to think it perfectly possible. "What breed?" he asked, apparently taking a mental note of it. He would probably prefer to supply some Manchurian caviare-eating variety, to keep up the tone of the hotel, but of course what I always want really is dear old Captain Jenks, gobbling his Whiskas far away in Wales.

SUSAN GEORGE
Actress

The thing I truly miss, is my Irish setters. I have always

dreamt of the day of running with them in the snow-covered mountains. But it is not to be, quarantine regulations make that an impossibility.

SALLY GUNNELL
Runner and Olympic Gold Medallist

When I travel, I miss home, my husband and my two cats —not in that order! When I was racing in Ghent earlier this year my black cat Demi went missing for 48 hours. My husband Jon eventually found her at the top of a tree and rescued her with the help of a very long ladder and a workman working nearby. All I could do was to hear the developments over the phone—Oh, how I wished I could have been at home to help with the hunt.

KEN LIVINGSTONE MP
Member of Parliament for Brent East

The things I miss most while travelling are comfort; peace and quiet; good food and sleep.

RICHARD BRIERS
Actor

I try not to travel too much because Fred, who is a mongrel and nearly thirteen years old, doesn't like it at all. I get a pretty dirty look if I'm away more than six hours!

JEFFREY BERNARD
Columnist

One of the things I really miss is a good cup of tea, in spite of my reputation—that may surprise you. The only place I've ever been to abroad where you can get a decent

cup of tea is the Muthaiga Club of *White Mischief* fame, in Kenya. It's like being in England—there are cucumber sandwiches, and Kenyan tea is the best, nicely strong. While in France they give you one teabag for the whole pot.

And I miss racing and cricket. In 1969 I bluffed my way into the British Consulate in Barcelona to get the result of the Derby. I said I had to make an urgent call, I had a very sick relative who might be dying. I rang my bookmaker and asked him to hold the telephone receiver out to the commentary. I backed the winner.

And I miss the newspapers—I'm addicted to newsprint, and don't want to pay a couple of quid for *The Times*.

11 Who eats what

Food Suitable for the Stores of Travellers.—The kinds of food that are the most portable in the ordinary sense of the term are:- Pemmican; meat-biscuit; dried meat; dried fish; wheat flour; biscuit; oatmeal; barley; peas; cheese; sugar; preserved potatoes; and Chollet's compressed vegetables.

Condiments.—The most portable and useful condiments for a traveller are—salt, red pepper, Harvey's sauce, lime-juice, dried onions, and curry powder. They should be bought at a first-rate shop; for red pepper, lime-juice, and curry-powder are often atrociously adulterated.

Art of Travel by Francis Galton, 1872

GEOFFREY MOORHOUSE
Writer and traveller

I've eaten sea slug in Guangzhou and raw, scarcely dead, goat in the Sahara, both times with qualms, but my queasiest digestive memory dates back to a journey up the Congo in a dugout.

I was with an African priest who was visiting some remote mission stations hundreds of miles above Kinshasa, and drums signalled our coming at every stage along the mighty river. The kindness of the people was overwhelming, and on the return journey our canoe was almost down to the gunnels under the load of presents we had been given, most of which was food. There was crocodile meat, and eggs, and fruit, and vegetables; and this packet of something parcelled up in a banana leaf—a glistening brown roly-poly object that I nearly dropped in disgust when I unwrapped it. But it was home-made peanut butter, the best I've ever tasted, superior in every way to anything you're likely to come across on the supermarket shelf. What you see isn't always what you get!

JILL DANDO
TV Presenter

I once did a holiday programme on behalf of Earthwatch. We were in the jungles of Nepal, living in a pretty unhealthy situation, and we were eating the local food, mainly goat and rice washed in dirty water. I really thought I was going to be ill. In fact, I was quite well, and only fell ill as a result of the flight home! Quite often it is better to eat the local food, rather than the food which is cooked to western styles in big expensive restaurants.

VALERIE SINGLETON

TV Presenter

The best food I've ever eaten abroad was some prawns—
probably the worst food I should eat. It was in Mexico,
and we all went down to what was hardly a village, just a
collection of huts and shacks, and sat in a very scruffy
cafe. I had the most wonderful prawns I've ever eaten,
and just tossed the shells onto the floor like everyone else,
no question of tidiness.

Being careful about food is so difficult—sometimes
you're safer with street food, than the buffet in the grand
hotel which has been sitiing around for hours. And what
do you do if you're hungry? It's often the spontaneous
things you eat which arc the best, eaten with local people.
Like delicious coconut milk on a hot Jamaican day when
we were filming in the middle of the fields with the cows.
Someone just lops the top off a coconut and hands it to
you. Or mango sliced for me on a Caribbean beach.

12 What cures who

Blistered Feet:—To prevent the feet from blistering, it is a good plan to soap the inside of the stocking before setting out, making a thick lather all over it. A raw egg broken into a boot before putting it on, greatly softens the leather.

Art of Travel by Francis Galton, 1872

MAUREEN LIPMAN
Actress and journalist

The only travel tip I can pass on to you was given to me by Bobby Charlton and Henry Cooper and that is to put brown wrapping paper, cut in the shape of an inner sole, inside your socks when travelling long distances. This avoids jet lag.

CHRIS BONINGTON
Mountaineer and writer

The most important quality for a mountaineer who wants to stay alive is a healthy sense of fear! This is the vital signal that things are getting dangerous. You can then make the choice of pressing that fear and deciding to push on or to answer it and turn back. The kind of person who never knows fear is the kind of person who gets killed in the mountains.

Staying healthy in the mountains is firstly a question of eating and particularly drinking enough. You need at least seven pints of liquid per day to avoid dehydration. It is also important to acclimatise properly giving your body time to adjust to the altitude. In this respect it is very important to be self-aware. If you get a violent headache, don't soldier on in silence but make sure you lose height immediately. Wait until the headache dies down before regaining altitude. Once again, a healthy sense of fear can help you stay alive.

RUPERT ALLASON MP
Member of Parliament and thriller writer

Before anyone goes abroad, they should go and get a prescription for an eye-drop called Otosporin. People often get Swimmer's Ear—it's a very common problem which

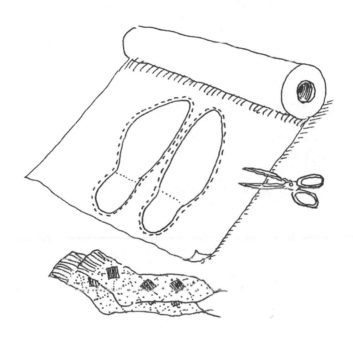

people get from swimming in polluted water like the Mediterranean. Children particularly get it, and I get it. But these eye-drops work brilliantly in the ear. I found this out on a Greek island where the chemist only had drugs that were seven years past the World Health Organisation sell-by date—and it worked wonders. I've talked to doctors about it and they absolutely approve it.

THE RT HON THE BARONESS CHALKER OF WALLASEY
Minister for Overseas Developement

As a frequent traveller, I always take a small phial of water purification drops in my travel bag. I have learned that it is better not to clean your teeth in beer or other bottled liquids.

THE DUCHESS OF BEAUFORT
Chatelaine and fund-raiser

I really do recommend testing mosquito repellent before buying or applying huge quantities. I once had a nasty experience in South America, deep in the Amazon Forest, when I discovered I was allergic to the only brand I had with me.

BERYL REID
Actress

I get hiccups when I am travelling and the best cure is to fill an egg cup with half water, half vinegar, and sip slowly. I don't know why it works, but it always does.

LULU
Singer

My travel tip for jet lag is to drink only water during the whole trip, and as little food as possible—certainly no stodge or carbohydrates. (I don't always manage to do this, but when I do it works wonders). Try it and see.

NICHOLAS PARSONS
TV and Radio Presenter

Always drink bottled water, even in the most hygienic hotels, until your stomach has become familiar with the natural impurities in the local water to which it is not conditioned. In some areas abroad, it is probably wiser never to drink the local water, if you want to be sure of enjoying your holiday.

JEREMY IRONS
Actor

To keep my health, I drink nothing but Coca-Cola which kills most tummy bugs before they have a chance to get excited.

13 Who loved what

General Remarks.—It is one of the most grateful results of a journey to the young traveller to find himself admitted, on the ground of having so much of special interest to relate, into the society of men with whose names he had long been familiar, and whom he had reverenced as his heroes.

Art of Travel by Francis Galton, 1872

DAVID WICKERS
Travel Correspondent, The Sunday Times

Sailing, many years ago, from Odessa on an overnight tub whose name I no longer recall, and nudging into Istanbul at first light, watching the sun float above the domes and minarets, listening to the throaty roar of early traffic and inhaling the shoreborne fragrances of freshly baked bread and spices, diesel fumes and fish, tobacco smoke and grilled lamb, lavatory and life.

THE RT HON. LORD SHACKELTON, KG, FRS
Explorer and author

In the course of the Oxford University Sarawak Expedition, 1931/32, I was attempting the first ascent of Mt. Mulu, a mountain which is a little under 8,000 feet high. The difficulty was alleged to be swamps and difficult climbing on the approach to Mt. Mulu. With the anxious support of the Penghulu (Chief), very unusual, I set out with 20 of his young head hunters and led by a rhinoceros hunter who had ascended the lower ridges and who acted as my guide. When, at the height of approximately 5,000 feet we were approaching the ridge leading to the summit, my companions of the Barawan tribe said they were frightened and did not want to go further up the mountain. There was a story of an *igok*, an animal which consumed any human being but left the unfortunate individual's hat!

After some difficulty, during which I announced that I was going alone, they decided to accompany me if they were allowed to carry out a sacrifice. They were cheerful pagans who carried out sacrifices, usually chickens, on any occasion and which they did not take too seriously. On this occasion, they carried out the ceremony using an egg (my last one). It was a dramatic moment and in the course of it the clouds fell so that all the mountains of Borneo, for many miles around, stood up in the dusk. I then had an extraordinary experience which I can only describe as a mystical one, when I felt exhilarated and able to do anything. It was a classic occasion for such an experience—shortage of food, anxiety and the extraordinary surroundings we were in. For two days I seemed to know everything, good and evil, but by the time I got to the top of the mountain (covered in rhododendrons) the experience had faded. I found it deeply moving at the time.

THE RT HON THE BARONESS CHALKER OF WALLASEY

Minister for Overseas Development

I believe my greatest travel experience must have been seeing Mount Everest at a height of more than 8,000 feet in the foothills in Nepal. The air was fresh, the magnificence of the mountains almost unbelievable, and I certainly felt 'on top of the world'.

LIZA GODDARD

Actress

We were staying in a plush hotel in Fiji, The Regent. The rooms were luxurious straw huts and all had picture windows opening onto the sand with a view of the sea and palm trees—idyllic. We decided to take a short boat trip to a small uninhabited island—within sight of the hotel. We were dropped on the island plus a packed lunch and the boat returned to the hotel with assurances of collecting us at 2 o' clock. We wandered around the island, investigating the handily placed Gents and Ladies wooden structures in the middle of the island.

Whilst paddling through the water, I encountered the only poisonous creature in Fiji - a small water snake, swimming towards me. I naturally screamed and leapt out of the water. Though apparently their jaws are too small to take a bite out of a human.

We had a lovely time but 2 o' clock came and went , so did 3 o' clock and 4 o' clock. Come 5 o' clock the wind had got up and still no sign of the boat. By now, we were beginning to worry. I reassuringly suggested we could all sleep in the loos—as one has to sleep off the sand because of the sand flea bites. While I was planning our night in the loo, my son Thom, calmly and sensibly, tied his sweatshirt to a stick and stood on the shore waving it.

Within 10 minutes we were rescued—the water by now very choppy. I was looking forward to a night out in our very own deserted desert island, but the children preferred dinner in the restaurant and sleep in the comfort of the hotel beds.

14 Who stays at home

Reluctant Servants:—They argue thus:-"Why should we do more than we knowingly undertook, and strain our constitutions and peril our lives in enterprises about which we are indifferent?"

Art of Travel by Francis Galton, 1872

RICHARD E GRANT
Actor

Never travel with a friend— you'll lose one.
Never travel without a loo-roll—you'll dream them.
Never wear open-toed sandals with socks unless with a vicar's convention, drink water in Cairo or queue for five hours to see Elvis' tomb in Memphis.
Never go "where none of the tourists go" unless you fancy meeting "yourself" in droves.

I long for a lunar landing tour.

KEITH WATERHOUSE
Writer

Never travel with anyone who holds conflicting views to yours about smoking, drinking, sunbathing, sightseeing, sex, shopping, punctuality, gregariousness, the importance of meals, the jollity of discos, the funniness of foreigners, of hygiene (personal and as regards washing lettuce). If the trip is self-catering, establish which self wil be doing the catering.

Couples of the opposite sex travelling together who do not have a cohabitation policy should establish one before they set off. Should they decide on a platonic expedition (and such things have been known) then they should be clear, if only tactitly so, whether either party is regarded as at liberty to take up with a foreigner of the worst sort.

Women travelling as a twosome, and who don't know each other that well, should agree in advance on the desirability or otherwise of chatting up ski instructors, beach boys and nice blokes at the next table. There should also be rules of etiquette in the event that one finds herself infatuated while the other doesn't.

GEORGE COLE
Actor

I loathe travelling. In fact, I am exactly like the character I played in *Root into Europe*. I do not travel well, and if possible would prefer not to travel at all. My advice is, don't eat rolls in France: you will break your teeth. And hang on to your wallet at Brussels airport: it will surely get lifted. All these things happened to me when I was forced to travel abroad making *Root*.

LEN DEIGHTON
Thriller writer

The best travel tip I can pass on to you is don't: stay at home, it's nicer. If someone says you must travel, get them to buy the ticket. If you have to pay, pay for it yourself, never pay the full fare. Devote a few hours of telephone time to seeking out the cheapest possible ticket.

Take a box of your own food: freshly cooked chicken or salmon, some perfect fruit and your favourite cheese. Take a calculator so you can work out how much extra you'd be paying per hour to sit somewhere up front where it is almost as hellish as it is back here. Give half of what you save to *Earthwatch*.

Index of Contributors

Join WEXAS, the UK's leading travel club for independent travellers

Established 1970

WEXAS, the publisher of *Around the World in 80 Ways*, has over 35,000 members. It offers substantial money-saving travel benefits. Here are just some of them:

* Scheduled airfares worldwide at reduced rates from London and other UK airports
* WEXAS lowest official airfare guarantee
* Global hotel discount programme of up to 55%
* Reductions on standard car rental rates up to 40 %
* Exclusive Round-the-World and Discoverers Tours brochures
* Free TRAVELLER magazine subscription
* Update - quarterly members' newsletter
* Directory of Membership Services - exclusive directory of travel benefits and savings
* The prize-winning *The Traveller's Handbook*

As a reader of *Around the World in 80 Ways*, you can receive one month's **FREE** membership.

Complete this coupon and **post today** for full details of membership.

Please send me, by return and without obligation, your FREE brochure. WEXAS International, 45 Brompton Road, London SW3 1DE

NAME (Mr/Mrs/Ms)_____

ADDRESS_____

_____

POSTCODE_____ COUNTRY_____

RECOMMEND A FRIEND
*AND GET A FREE 876-PAGE
TRAVELLER'S HANDBOOK*

Established 1970

As a member of the UK's premier travel club you are already aware of the many money-saving benefits and travel services offered by **WEXAS**.

If you know of someone who would like to receive more information about **WEXAS**, simply complete the name and address details on this form, return it to us and we'll do the rest by sending full membership details.

Each new member joining as a result of your recommendation will receive a free copy of the new edition of *The Traveller's Handbook* - and so will you!

Complete this coupon and **post today** so that your friend can receive membership details.

- -

YOUR FRIEND'S NAME AND ADDRESS
Please send details of WEXAS to:

NAME (Mr/Mrs/Ms)_____
ADDRESS_____
_____
POSTCODE_____ COUNTRY_____

YOUR NAME AND MEMBERSHIP NUMBER

NAME (MR/MRS/MS)_____
MEMBERSHIP NUMBER _ _ _ _ _ _

WEXAS International, 45 Brompton Road, London SW3 1DE